*GREATER THAN A T
   ALSO AVAILABL.
        AUDIOBOOK FORMAT.

Greater Than a Tourist Book Series Reviews from Readers

I think the series is wonderful and beneficial for tourists to get information before visiting the city.

-Seckin Zumbul, Izmir Turkey

I am a world traveler who has read many trip guides but this one really made a difference for me. I would call it a heartfelt creation of a local guide expert instead of just a guide.

-Susy, Isla Holbox, Mexico

New to the area like me, this is a must have!

-Joe, Bloomington, USA

This is a good series that gets down to it when looking for things to do at your destination without having to read a novel for just a few ideas.

-Rachel, Monterey, USA

Good information to have to plan my trip to this destination.

-Pennie Farrell, Mexico

Great ideas for a port day.

-Mary Martin USA

Aptly titled, you won't just be a tourist after reading this book. You'll be greater than a tourist!

-Alan Warner, Grand Rapids, USA

Even though I only have three days to spend in San Miguel in an upcoming visit, I will use the author's suggestions to guide some of my time there. An easy read - with chapters named to guide me in directions I want to go.

-Robert Catapano, USA

Great insights from a local perspective! Useful information and a very good value!

-Sarah, USA

This series provides an in-depth experience through the eyes of a local. Reading these series will help you to travel the city in with confidence and it'll make your journey a unique one.

-Andrew Teoh, Ipoh, Malaysia

>TOURIST

GREATER THAN A TOURIST- MALMO SWEDEN

50 Travel Tips from a Local

Okezi O Otuoba

Greater Than a Tourist-Malmo Sweden   Copyright © 2021 by CZYK Publishing LLC. All Rights Reserved.

All rights reserved. No part of this book may be reproduced in any form or by any electronic or mechanical means including information storage and retrieval systems, without permission in writing from the author. The only exception is by a reviewer, who may quote short excerpts in a review.

The statements in this book are of the authors and may not be the views of CZYK Publishing or Greater Than a Tourist.

First Edition

Cover designed by: Ivana Stamenkovic

Cover Image: https://pixabay.com/photos/simrishamn-sk%C3%A5ne-sweden-malm%C3%B6-4543825/

Image 1: By User Jorchr on sv.wikipedia - Jorchr, CC BY-SA 3.0, https://commons.wikimedia.org/w/index.php?curid=1099061

Image 2: By Fpo74 - Own work, CC BY-SA 3.0, https://commons.wikimedia.org/w/index.php?curid=13245577

Image 3: Public Domain, https://commons.wikimedia.org/w/index.php?curid=365042

Image 4: By Fred J - Own work, CC BY 1.0, https://commons.wikimedia.org/w/index.php?curid=129374

CZYK
PUBLISHING

CZYK Publishing Since 2011.
CZYKPublishing.com
Greater Than a Tourist

Lock Haven, PA
All rights reserved.
ISBN: 9798510049176

>TOURIST

50 TRAVEL TIPS FROM A LOCAL

BOOK DESCRIPTION

With travel tips and culture in our guidebooks written by a local, it is never too late to visit Malmo. Greater Than a Tourist- Malmo, Sweden by Author Okezi O Otuoba, offers the inside scoop on Malmo. Most travel books tell you how to travel like a tourist. Although there is nothing wrong with that, as part of the 'Greater Than a Tourist' series, this book will give you candid travel tips from someone who has lived at your next travel destination. This guide book will not tell you exact addresses or store hours but instead gives you knowledge that you may not find in other smaller print travel books. Experience cultural, culinary delights, and attractions with the guidance of a Local. Slow down and get to know the people with this invaluable guide. By the time you finish this book, you will be eager and prepared to discover new activities at your next travel destination.

Inside this travel guide book you will find:

  Visitor information from a Local
  Tour ideas and inspiration
  Save time with valuable guidebook information

Greater Than a Tourist- A Travel Guidebook with 50 Travel Tips from a Local. Slow down, stay in one place, and get to know the people and culture. By the time you finish this book, you will be eager and prepared to travel to your next destination.

>TOURIST

OUR STORY

Traveling is a passion of the Greater than a Tourist book series creator. Lisa studied abroad in college, and for their honeymoon Lisa and her husband toured Europe. During her travels to Malta, an older man tried to give her some advice based on his own experience living on the island since he was a young boy. She was not sure if she should talk to the stranger but was interested in his advice. When traveling to some places she was wary to talk to locals because she was afraid that they weren't being genuine. Through her travels, Lisa learned how much locals had to share with tourists. Lisa created the Greater Than a Tourist book series to help connect people with locals. A topic that locals are very passionate about sharing.

>TOURIST

TABLE OF CONTENTS

Book Description

Our Story

Table of Contents

Dedication

About the Author

How to Use This Book

From the Publisher

WELCOME TO > TOURIST

1. Welcome to Malmo, Did You Bring Your Umbrella and Raincoat?
2. Can You Ride a Bicycle? Start Practicing If You Can't.
3. Fika Fika Fika …... Just Fika It.
4. Call Me a Falafel Fan, I Don't Care.
5. Green or Yellow, What's Your Location?
6. I Love Fish…… Do you?
7. Second Hand Shops…. Best Value for Your Money.
8. Art Lover? Get Over Here Let's Go See Street Arts.
9. Where Are My African Folks? This Is for You…...
10. Swedish Coffee …… A Trial Will Convince You.
11. Euphoria…. Oh!!! Sorry, It's Called Emporia.

12. Have You Met My Neighbors? You Should...
13. Roll Roll Roll Your Boat, Gentle Down the Stream...
14. Not All Those Who Wander Are Lost .... J R R Tolkien.
15. Google Knows It All ......
16. P-A-R-K-S ...
17. I Think I'm Going to Puke... One Man's Food Is Another Man's Poison.
18. Life Is a Gamble, Come On!! Roll The Dice.
19. A Blast from The Past ...
20. A Wonder in The Sky... That Turns with Pride.
21. Hej!! what-Sup Malmö?
22. Declare The Past, Diagnose The Present, Foretell The Future - Hippocrates.
23. Padlocks of Love....
24. Here Is My Heart, Here Is My History, Here Is My Game, Take It Further. - Zlatan.
25. Fun Is Spelled .... S - U - M - M - E - R.
26. Technology and Maritime Museum.
27. What A Day!! I Need to Go to Bed.
28. You May Sit in Our Library and Yet Be in All Quarters of the Earth... John Lubbock.
29. Paint Your Emotions....
30. Sky Above, Sun On My Face, Sand Below, Peace Within....

>TOURIST

31. A Day at The Zoo...
32. Just Breathe....
33. Stay On the Queue.
34. It's Friday and I'm Ready to Swing...
35. J-U-N-G-L-E
36. I Found the Perfect Gift.
37. Art Is Wonder...
38. Sticking to My Candy Crush.
39. Book A Tour...
40. Count The Memories, Not The Calories.
41. Rent A Car, And Explore.
42. A Quiet Time and Place.
43. A Slice of Culture, Customs and Etiquette.
44. The Most Expensive Noise.
45. Either Give Me More Wine or Leave Me Alone. - Rumi
46. We Are All Mad Here.
47. Let's Go Get Some Groceries.
48. Choco. la. ta.
49. Swedish Identity.
50. Dancing Round the Maypole.

TOP REASONS TO BOOK THIS TRIP

Packing and Planning Tips

Travel Questions

Travel Bucket List

NOTES

DEDICATION

This book is dedicated to my daughter Frances Ewomazino Otuoba. Her love for traveling and trying out new things is amazing; her creativity is just about to hit the world... may all your dreams come to pass.

"With age comes wisdom, with travels comes understanding."
Sandra Lake

ABOUT THE AUTHOR

Okezi is a wife, mother, a poet, and a freelance writer from Nigeria currently residing in Malmo, Sweden. She is a thespian and currently pursuing her master degree in culture and change. She loves to cook and spends endless hours writing poems. She also likes trying out new cuisines and taking pictures while traveling and having new experiences.

>TOURIST

HOW TO USE THIS BOOK

The *Greater Than a Tourist* book series was written by someone who has lived in an area for over three months. The goal of this book is to help travelers either dream or experience different locations by providing opinions from a local. The author has made suggestions based on their own experiences. Please check before traveling to the area in case the suggested places are unavailable.

Travel Advisories: As a first step in planning any trip abroad, check the Travel Advisories for your intended destination.
https://travel.state.gov/content/travel/en/traveladvisories/traveladvisories.html

FROM THE PUBLISHER

Traveling can be one of the most important parts of a person's life. The anticipation and memories that you have are some of the best. As a publisher of the Greater Than a Tourist, as well as the popular *50 Things to Know* book series, we strive to help you learn about new places, spark your imagination, and inspire you. Wherever you are and whatever you do I wish you safe, fun, and inspiring travel.

Lisa Rusczyk Ed. D.
CZYK Publishing

>TOURIST

```
WELCOME TO
> TOURIST
```

>TOURIST

Pildammsparken with the old water tower

The Øresund Bridge, connecting Malmö to Copenhagen and the Scandinavian peninsula with Central Europe through Denmark.

Malmö's old city hall.

St. Peter's Church in Malmö

>TOURIST

Traveling - It leaves you speechless then turns you into a storyteller

- Ibn Battuta

For anyone who has had the privilege of being raised in Nigeria, the most populous black nation on the face of Mother Earth, a country with the largest ethnic group with centuries of historical cultures, traditions and incredible sites littered everywhere. The evidence of this abounds in the various rich experiences which is clearly reflected in cultural and historical relevance of my days back in Nigeria and has given me the urge to explore Malmo which is Sweden's third largest city and a multicultural portal to Europe, despite its modern exteriors it's filled with history, mix architectural styles and ethnic restaurants scattered around.

There are no surprises that a change of environment increases happiness and excitement to explore.

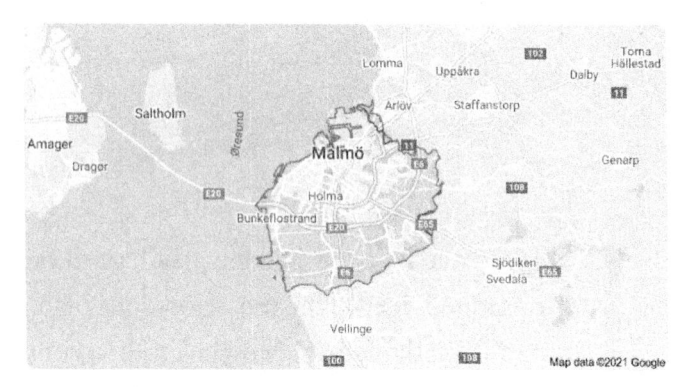

Malmö Municipality
Sweden

>TOURIST

Malmo Sweden Climate

	High	Low
January	38	30
February	38	29
March	44	32
April	55	38
May	64	45
June	68	52
July	73	56
August	71	56
September	65	50
October	54	43
November	46	37
December	40	32

GreaterThanaTourist.com

Temperatures are in Fahrenheit degrees.
Source: NOAA

>TOURIST

1. WELCOME TO MALMO, DID YOU BRING YOUR UMBRELLA AND RAINCOAT?

No matter the season, anytime you are coming to Malmo bring an umbrella or raincoat and a sweater. in Malmo during the entire year the rain falls. You can be out on a very hot summer day and before you know it the skies start taking a shower. be prepared always.

2. CAN YOU RIDE A BICYCLE? START PRACTICING IF YOU CAN'T.

It is such a lovely city to ride a bike which is very common in Sweden especially Malmo, because the city is compact and the land is pretty flat, it makes sense to get around on 2 wheels, with well parted paths for bicycles and scooters which you can get almost everywhere in the city for rent with a very cheap amount. But if you can't ride a bike, don't worry because with such short walks or exploring you can visit most of the fun places in the city without stress.

3. FIKA FIKA FIKA ...... JUST FIKA IT.

Fika is a Swedish culture and in Malmo it has become a ritual. So whenever you visit Malmo don't be surprised to see people gathered around cafes even in working hours drinking coffee and eating cake. Fika is called coffee and cake break, taking time out of a busy day schedule to have a hot cup of coffee and something sweet or a slice of cake with friends and colleagues in a cafe or home for about a half hour, it's usually a time to focus on yourself and others. so be prepared to just sit and talk over a cup of coffee and cake. It's one of the most interesting things to do in Malmo.

>TOURIST

4. CALL ME A FALAFEL FAN, I DON'T CARE.

Are you a vegetarian? if yes, then you will definitely enjoy your stay here. Malmo is an ecologically healthy city filled with great food, especially lots of vegan options. Falafel has become a symbol in Malmo, best in the whole of Sweden, with cheap falafel stands around the city. It is a Middle Eastern food brought to Malmo by immigrants from Lebanon and Israel. It is cheap and yet you get a value for your money. so delicious and made of ground chickpea, herbs and spices which is then formed into balls and deep fried, you can have it with Kebab if you are not a vegetarian, it's so tasty and a must try whenever you visit Malmo. Falafel gives you a sense of the community. It's funny how a ball of fried chickpeas becomes a symbol for Malmo.

5. GREEN OR YELLOW, WHAT'S YOUR LOCATION?

Public Transportation in Malmo is very cheap and efficient. Taxis are very expensive, so stick to the buses or trains. In Malmo there are two types of bus, we have the green and the yellow and these are operated by Skanetrafiken. The green takes you within Malmo city and then the yellow takes you on regional journeys to places around Malmo like Helsingborg and Ystad. Be prepared because you can't buy a ticket aboard, so you need to download the app at the Appstore or Play Store or better still get one at the Skanetrafiken outlet in Central station or the JoJo card which is cheaper and flexible for tourists. I forgot to mention the free wireless internet network available in all the buses and trains around the city.

6. I LOVE FISH...... DO YOU?

Are you a Fish lover? If yes, then you should sit back and enjoy this ride by paying a visit to the popular Fiskehoddorna which is called the fish market. You can't come to Malmo and miss this place, where you can eat homemade local fish and chips in a garden with a great view of the fishing huts and I must confess, it's a great place for nice pictures.

7. SECOND HAND SHOPS.... BEST VALUE FOR YOUR MONEY.

Shopping in Malmo is relatively expensive but thanks to second hand shops all over the city where you can get things for a really cheap amount. In the whole of Sweden second hand shops are available because apart from the fact that it helps in saving money it has a reduced impact on the environment in terms of recycling and reuse of items which is a wide spread message in Sweden, and these shops are common in Malmo. It is so much fun shopping in a secondhand shop because you find some interesting, unique and weird things that you wouldn't find in ordinary shops. It is super entertaining going round the shops and seeing things that are uncommon, ranging from furniture, clothing, old rare objects Et al. I actually got my first winter jacket from a second hand shop and it was less than half the price of a new one and indeed the best value for my money.

8. ART LOVER? GET OVER HERE LET'S GO SEE STREET ARTS.

My love for art is overwhelming and street arts or graffiti is just a wonder to behold. Malmo has loads of street art in corners around the city. Most times I wonder when they were actually drawn and I always pray to run into them. Walking down the road to get groceries is always fun for me because I get to walk along this long wall filled with art and before I know it I am at my destination. It's a lovely place to take pictures and also helps you in finding your way when you are lost, each time you see one you just know wherever you pass that same place. it helps, i can tell you that.

9. WHERE ARE MY AFRICAN FOLKS? THIS IS FOR YOU......

You are far from home and tired of the food here in Malmo and you are an African especially those from Nigeria, I have got good news for you and I am so excited about this particular topic because when I got to Malmo after few months I got home sick and started missing my native food but when I found out the number of African shops available in the city I was overwhelmed. A trip there and my homesick problem was solved, all my local, native food and ingredients were in abundance for body lotions and hair products. I was finally able to solve my hair problem which was a major setback for me due to location and weather. If you must know, I have natural dreadlocks and each hair salon I went to in Malmo seemed not to understand how to treat my hair, until I found an African shop and most of them have salons attached and my hair was rescued. I forgot to mention that it is very expensive, yes it is, and it is still a mystery to me.

10. SWEDISH COFFEE ...... A TRIAL WILL CONVINCE YOU.

Malmo, the southern city of Sweden is the supplier of the best coffee in the country. if you love coffee then I guess you will have it first hand in Malmo. Before I left Nigeria I have always longed to have a taste of Swedish coffee and the first time I tasted it I couldn't finish a cup even after adding lots of milk and sugar. That was my experience and am waiting to hear yours after trying it. Indeed, a trial will convince you to keep on drinking it or stop you from drinking it like it did to me. I guess my experience was due to the fact that I come from a non-coffee drinking country and even when we want to drink coffee it must be really creamy and sweet or better still we stick to cocoa.

11. EUPHORIA.... OH!!! SORRY, IT'S CALLED EMPORIA.

The almighty Emporia, that's how I call it. One of the biggest shopping malls in Scandinavia and yes!! It's situated in Malmo. It's indeed a wonder to behold, the size is an equivalent to four soccer fields in total with over two hundred shops located inside. My first visit to Emporia was actually by mistake, I was just a week old in Malmö and I got lost on my way somewhere and while sitting in the bus we approached this gigantic magnificent building, I came down from the bus and ran into the shopping mall with excitement…. When I finally got home I was under the euphoria of Emporia for days. Each time I

>TOURIST

go there it feels like I'm just visiting it for the first time. You should give it a try too, great shops where you can find everything from clothes to coffee, food, live plants, and playground for kids and remember to come with your credit card most shops don't accept cash.

12. HAVE YOU MET MY NEIGHBORS? YOU SHOULD...

Do you know that Malmo is just a few minutes away from Denmark? It's so interesting to know that within a few hours you can visit two countries without breaking the bank. And this is where i am going to introduce to you the Oresund Bridge (Oresundsbron), it is Europe's longest road/rail bridge, its fifteen minutes' drive from Malmo and this bridge links Sweden and Denmark, it is multi-faceted, a railway, road and a tunnel. you can take a trip to Copenhagen airport Denmark across the bridge through the tunnel from Malmo using the train lines and city buses which belong to Skanetrafiken as well as Oresund trains at a very cheap cost. If you come to Malmo during summer time, then you are in luck because you can get summer tickets at a very cheap price from the Skanetrafiken app and just sit and relax while you go round the city and cross over the Oresund Bridge without stress. And don't forget to say hi to my neighbors.

13. ROLL ROLL ROLL YOUR BOAT, GENTLE DOWN THE STREAM...

If you see a crocodile don't forget to scream... I miss kindergarten and I also miss boat rides. Growing up in the southern part of Nigeria which is filled with water I have great experience from the Niger Delta region, boat fishing and transportation to most villages that cannot be accessed by road and this has fueled my love for boat rides. So if you love boat rides too then you are in the best part of Sweden, the southern part of the country with lots of canal and boat ride experiences. The best way to see Malmö is from the water and you have lots of canal and boat rentals, just go online book a boat Malmö and voila!! for a cheap price you can rent one, come with your food and drinks and enjoy Malmo from the canals, and yes!! you can Fika on your boat ride. You can also ferry between Helsingborg and Helsingor. book a boat tour and enjoy The Gondola Malmo.

14. NOT ALL THOSE WHO WANDER ARE LOST .... J R R TOLKIEN.

I am sorry to burst your bubbles, when I arrived in Malmo it was the other way around, I was a lost girl who became a wanderer. Each time I go out I get lost and begin to wander. Let me be frank with you, getting lost in Malmo is a must, just hold on and I will tell you why.

My first three months in Malmo was really an adventure, some days I cried and other days I laughed so hard at myself. I guess you are wondering why, do not blame me, but blame the bus stations, bus numbers, and positions which are kind of tricky, their names are jaw breaking, you never can pronounce most of them so just leave it to the Swedes to pronounce. Let me give you a tip that helped me, it's stressful and time consuming but helpful in getting to know the city quickly. when you ask for directions most times you end up getting lost the more due to communication, most persons you meet out there can't really express themselves in English well enough and the way they pronounce these words are totally different from the way an English speaking person will pronounce them and again most Swedes are very quiet and withdrawn and Sometimes get scared when you approach them for directions…..so what i did each time i got lost and couldn't find my way was to always take a bus to Malmo central station and ran over to the Skanetrafiken office for directions or go through the app and locate the bus right there because all the buses convey at the central station.

15. GOOGLE KNOWS IT ALL

If google was human he would have long been dead, from stress i guess. Coming from a country like Nigeria where google maps and translator isn't really a thing except for those living in the big cities. Getting to Malmo one thing you can't do without is a google translator and map, you just have to befriend google to be able to go round the city especially for those riding bikes and walking. Most signs are in

>TOURIST

Swedish so all you do is use your camera to scan and translate. I still do it till date. Even in supermarkets most product manuals are written in Swedish and all I do is scan and translate. Most Swedes are fluent in English but Malmo is a small city and most people you find can't really express themselves in English even if they understand and write in English.

16. P-A-R-K-S ...

Malmo is a city well known for its beautiful and fun parks. There are so many parks in Malmo and there is one common thing about all of them and that is the touch of nature, ranging from beautiful flowers to ponds and ducks to feed. A visit to Malmo and a stroll in the city parks is something you won't forget in a hurry. They are many, but you can't come to Malmo and not visit the oldest park called The Kings Park (Kungsparken), it's such a peaceful place to relax, inspired by English garden, old trees, lush lawns, ponds and ducks to feed and my favorite is the vaulted caves. Each Time I visit Kings park it reminds me of London. Now let me tell you about my favorite park in Malmo, it's called Folkets Park also known as The People's Park, the favorite destination for locals and tourists especially for families, if you are visiting Malmo with kids then this is a place you want to visit. All kids in Malmo love Folket Park, it's filled with fun games, green area ponds and ice cream stands, all kinds of sculptures, eateries, and even outdoor stage space with free live music Et al.... all for free, but you have to pay for your food.

17. I THINK I'M GOING TO PUKE... ONE MAN'S FOOD IS ANOTHER MAN'S POISON.

Forgive my manners in dealing with this topic, while I introduce to you Disgusting Food Museum, situated in no other place but Malmo. Are you curious about food from exotic cultures? Do you love to explore the world of food to challenge your notion on what is and what isn't edible? Do you dare to smell the world's stinkiest cheese or taste sweets made with metal cleansing chemicals? If your answer is yes then the best place to visit while in Malmo is the Disgusting Food Museum, whose aim is educating people to have a more open mind about food culture from around the world, exhibiting about 80 of the world's most disgusting foods. Here is a tip for you, try to book tickets online ahead of time to secure a spot because it can be crowded most times, it's not so expensive. Do you want my opinion? Why do I have to pay to smell and see disgusting food? And please don't forget to put some coffee seeds in a small container so you can smell it afterwards, I heard it eliminates smell from the nostrils.

18. LIFE IS A GAMBLE, COME ON!! ROLL THE DICE.

I am not a fan of Casinos but I sure do enjoy magic performances, either way you are going to enjoy a day at the casino in Malmo, a touch of Las Vegas in the city. and the place to be is Casino Cosmopol Malmo, which is few minutes' walk away from the central station and its located inside Kings Park (Kungsparken), after a walk in the park you can pay a visit to the casino with a fee, you must be 20 years or older with an ID and passport and must be prepared to have your picture taken, because all visitors are photographed before entry, the best part of the experience is the in house magician who goes around performing tricks and creating comic relief to ease tension. Here are some tips to help you, dress smart and clean, no smoking allowed inside the casino, and the prices of drinks are high so be prepared.

19. A BLAST FROM THE PAST
●●●

The city of Malmo has everything it takes to wow tourists and if you are a lover of history, especially Swedish history then you should visit the Historic Malmo Castle (Malmohus Slott), an amazing atmosphere perceived by the spirits of ancient ages. It is a place where several of the city's major museums are housed, a mix of little of this and little of that. Inside you find Malmo Museum of Art, Small Aquarium, City Museum, and The Natural History Museum. The castle was built in 1537 to 1542, it's the oldest preserved renaissance castle in Scandinavia. My first trip to Malmohus I spent 4 hours exploring without even knowing, I guess time flies when you are having fun. inside is simply magical with lots of rare creatures and aquatic animals, lots of exciting exhibitions where you learn a bit of history (post-war

Sweden) and Art Expo, and am so excited to inform you that there is something for everybody, so the kids can also have fun. It's very affordable with such a great value for your money and a must see. you should try visiting Malmohus at night, where lights are projecting images of medieval parties happening inside the castle on outside windows. It's a sight to behold, and lastly there's a very good restaurant inside with a very rich menu and modest prices.

20. A WONDER IN THE SKY... THAT TURNS WITH PRIDE.

Introducing the Turning Torso, the pride of Malmo city, the most attractive place in Malmo, the World's first twisted skyscraper and the tallest building in Scandinavia with a height of 190m and the building is powered with locally produced renewable energy. The Turning Torso is indeed a masterpiece, awesome, beautiful and an impressive architectural gem in Sweden. permit me to show it off a little bit, in 2005 it won the Gold Emporis Skyscraper Award and then in 2015 The Turning Torso was also the winner of the 10-year Award from the Council of Tall Buildings and Urban Habitats.

The building clearly dominates the rather soulless modern quarter of the city with its Neo Futuristic design, a place where every architect should visit at least once. Each time I pass the building I always whisper a note of thanks to Santiago Calatrava the architect of the wonder in the form of a building. If you are visiting Sweden for the first time you should take a trip to Malmo and see this wonder. It is pretty easy to get to using mass transportation and a lovely site for pictures. The view from the observation deck on the 49th floor is breathtaking, the 53rd and 54th floors are only opened to the public on certain days.

21. HEJ!! WHAT-SUP MALMÖ?

Are you a risk taker and not scared of water? Never mind, this question is irrelevant, because I am a risk taker and not scared of water but i have never thought of trying this. Maybe I will try it this summer when I finally beat my fears. What-Sup Malmö is a stand up paddling tour for all levels, so much awaits you in this adventurous tour where you book a stand up paddle board and go round the city of Malmo Suping. It's such an amazing way to experience the

>TOURIST

sunset with such breathtaking views, be prepared to get wet and maybe a little sunburned and loads of fun. it is ok to be scared at first, but the guides will take away your fears by giving you useful tips before you get on board, it's easy to book online just send a message, and you will get yourself a paddle board and a great host, who has great passion for Suping and very pedagogical. and this is my favorite part, you can get an extra discount if you pick up trash during you tour… thank me later.

22. DECLARE THE PAST, DIAGNOSE THE PRESENT, FORETELL THE FUTURE – HIPPOCRATES.

I present to you, Apoteket Lejonet Malmo. Sweden's oldest pharmacy, a nice old fashioned pharmacy with modern drugs. This oldest operating pharmacy is located in the old part of the city with its original essence preserved, with stunning decorations, extremely beautiful for taking pictures. it's not only a pharmacy but also a museum. You should definitely see this when visiting Malmo, the building makes the place look expensive, but the products are cheaper inside compared to other pharmacies. next to it is the commercial passage that connects with the street of the theatre and the church of San Pedro, the oldest in the city. This historical pharmacy has a nice balcony where shelves with antique bottles are kept on the 2nd floor of the building. The staff are friendly and fluent in English. so if you get a bit stressed due to your tour and a bit uncomfortable due to the different cuisines, this is the best place to visit, while getting you drugs your tour continues. one learns a great deal sometimes from being sick.

23. PADLOCKS OF LOVE....

Love is the greatest gift of all and it makes us do crazy things. Are you in love, and visiting Malmo with your partner? or are you thinking of proposing? I wish you could see me right now while writing this, just blushing like a girl who just had her first kiss. I present to you, Malmo Titanic Lovelock Point, the most romantic place in Malmo. This is where all the fun people, especially those in love go to, with a unique scenic view of the coastline, the Oresundsbron and the Turning Torso. You can sit and relax while you chat with your partner and watch people sing or teach something with full talent. a very lovely place for pictures and one of the best places for marriage proposals. It's also a super fun place to jump into water but you have to be careful when jumping because the water is not too deep so you don't fall too hard and hurt yourself. when visiting try to keep warm it's pretty cold out there and the best part of this place is that you can do the titanic scene here with your lover, and don't forget to come with a padlock to lock your love forever. The first time I visited this place I was amazed at the number of padlocks I saw. Truly, love makes us do crazy things.

24. HERE IS MY HEART, HERE IS MY HISTORY, HERE IS MY GAME, TAKE IT FURTHER. - ZLATAN.

If you are a lover of football with a rich tradition then you must visit Malmo, the home of Zlatan, an enigma who won league titles with 6 different countries and countless other honors and also home of Malmö Fotbollförening, commonly known as Malmö FF, the most successful football club in Sweden, with many trophies won. Malmo FF are based at the Eleda Stadium in Malmo, the UEFA category 4 rated Stadium, it's a must see, the club have won a record Swedish Championship Titles and the most National Cup Titles and it's the richest football club in Sweden. Now let's go deeper, if you are a fan of Zlatan Ibrahimović, then you can't come to Malmo and not visit Zlatan Court, it's a football field located in Rosengard which happens to be my neighborhood, it's such an interesting part of the area, with youths playing football and aspiring to become like Zlatan, the field was dedicated and inaugurated by him in 2007, it lies in the courtyard of Cronmas Vag where Zlatan used to play football during his childhood days. The pitch is made of recycled athletic shoes, the field is illuminated during dark hours, so don't worry if you get there at night, you can still have nice pictures taken and a lovely view too. on the ground is the footprints and autograph of Zlatan which has been immortalized in a star shaped impression at the pitch, his golden silhouette welcomes you to the mid field and the best part of it is the entrance of the court where you have the inscriptions, HERE IS MY HEART, HERE IS MY HISTORY, HERE IS MY GAME, TAKE IT FURTHER. - ZLATAN. It's really worth visiting, just to see with your eyes how far work passion and commitment can bring you to the limelight. If you love soccer, it's a place you must visit in Malmo and it's easy to get there. It's just a straight bus from central station, the popular bus 5.

25. FUN IS SPELLED …. S - U - M - M - E - R.

Malmo is indeed a very happy place, home of the friendliest people in Sweden. It was named the happiest city in Sweden in 2016. The Swedish people are naturally very reserved but the famous reserve life is in short supply here in our small populated city of about 400,000 people who are made up of more than 200 nationalities and this is the reason why Malmo has a rich cultural life, mix architectural styles, picturesque city parks, cutting edge arts to see and exhibits through provoking museums. Summer in Malmo is the best I have experienced and one of the best in the whole of Sweden, filled with different activities from different cultures. you can get a free walking tour to some very interesting parts of the town, my best part of summer is street food and desserts, wow, i can never get over that part, summer in Malmo feels like Christmas in Nigeria, you see people all round eating different cuisines, down the lake you can also indulge in sunset fishing, hiking and beach parties and for those who wants to take it further, you can go for Adrenaline and Extreme sightseeing tours by Flyby Events, and for those who wants to go countryside can visit the Kummingarden Ridlekis for horse riding tours, live concerts and city tours with bikes, the list is endless, summer is a blast in Malmö and the most interesting part of it all is the summer tickets for all city buses, regional buses and train lines which belongs to Skanetrafiken as well as Oresund trains to go to Copenhagen international airport Denmark. you can get it at a very cheap rate to tour round the city, just download the Skanetrafiken App on App Store or Play Store and you are all set. Sadly, summer in Sweden is short but pleasant and busy, colorful not too cold but dark autumns and lovely but kind of hit and miss springs, but in all, always remember to go out with your umbrella and coat, it rains in Malmo all seasons.

>TOURIST

26. TECHNOLOGY AND MARITIME MUSEUM.

The great science and technology museum located in Malmo is the best place to be especially in bad weather, known for its indoor playground basement for adults and kids, such a great place to be in winter. There are so many fun activities in place for visitors, fantastic photo exhibitions, walking through a real submarine, exhibition of old cars and planes, such an interesting museum about the old days. The most fascinating and educating part of it is the Anthropocene exhibit about humans' large scale impact on Earth. you can bring your own Fika to enjoy in the lounge next to the play area while you watch your kids play. It's really interactive and very cheap, and the best part is that you can also use the ticket to get into Malmohus which is the Historic Malmo Castle.

27. WHAT A DAY!! I NEED TO GO TO BED.

Cost of living in Malmo is less expensive than most cities both in Sweden and some other parts of the world, with high quality of living in a very affordable cost, environmentally friendly city with everything you need just a walk or quick bike away. Rental prices are significantly cheaper than those in Stockholm and Gothenburg, as a tourist if you are visiting Malmo for the first time just be rest assured you are going to enjoy your stay no matter your budget or taste. I am going to start from the high rise, staying downtown in the city center is the best, with different tourist attractions to see with ease, with lots of convenient hotels, you can also get pet friendly hotels, I love the sound of luxury. but don't worry the city got you covered, Malmo has few budget options which are also in good locations near the Malmo Arena, where you have the Best Western Malmo Arena Hotel, best value for your money, with a train service straight to city center, and for those with a lower budget like students can also enjoy their stay at the STF Malmo city Hotel which offers basic rooms and shared rooms. Football fans can also enjoy their stay by lodging near the stadium with a view of the pitch. I forgot to mention that most hotels give free breakfast and yes!! all hotels have free WIFI connections.

28. YOU MAY SIT IN OUR LIBRARY AND YET BE IN ALL QUARTERS OF THE EARTH... JOHN LUBBOCK.

Let's take our tour a little further into a place I call paradise. If you are a lover of books, then this place is definitely worth stopping by for a sneak peek or better still put to good use. I present to you, Malmo City Library (Malmo Stadsbibliotek), a public library, one of the best in Sweden and the first library to lend video games in the country. The building is magnificently beautiful and features floor to ceiling windows with a view overlooking a park. Such an amazing Architecture which shows the multicultural environment that shapes Malmo to the ever changing city. A Mixture of old and new and a nice place for great pictures. There is a cafe downstairs and a special place for kids to play and read. a membership card is easy to get, just in a few minutes and you can actually borrow a book for 28 days. Let me give you a tip, you can actually make photocopies of documents inside the library, or just go in there and use the internet, whatever your mission there you will definitely enjoy your visit.

29. PAINT YOUR EMOTIONS....

I love to paint, it's something I do when I get really sad and lonely, it helps me find relief, I guess it's therapeutic. When I got to Malmo a friend of mine introduced me to an art cafe called MADE ME. It's a ceramic painting cafe where you design or paint ceramics. You should visit this place wherever you come to Malmo and put your creative skills to good use. you can come along with your friends and family, especially kids. Here is how it works: first you book a table or drop in during opening hours, choose your ceramic item to paint, and paint your item, collect finished items days later when they are done glazing it. you don't have to be a pro, just paint or play with colors. The fun part of it is that all these are for a reasonable price, with all materials and great selections of items to paint included. Did I mention the free coffee? ok!! I just did. More importantly you can design any ceramic and take it back home as a souvenir for those you left at home or for yourself.

30. SKY ABOVE, SUN ON MY FACE, SAND BELOW, PEACE WITHIN....

Life they say is a Beach, find your wave. I found mine in the city of Malmo, the city of bathers, canals, seas, beautiful sandy and clean beaches. 20 minutes from the city Centre to Ribersborg and there you will find the most beautiful sight to behold, RIBERSBORG BEACH. you can't come to Malmo and not visit this place, it's a place where everyone from around the world have fun and enjoy swimming especially during summer, sun bathing and lazing around and its known for its long stretch of sand, perfect for kids due to shallow areas, and excellent views of Turning Torso and Oresund Bridge, with play areas, barbecue spots and cafes. Let me introduce my favorite part, which is called RIBERSBORGS KALLBADHUS. It's a sea water bathing facility, an open public bath located right there at Ribersborgs Beach, with saunas and warm bathtubs. Come closer let me tell you a secret, there is a nude bathing facility in there with separate male and female saunas, and the LGBT community affected by gender restrictions are not left out too, they have their dedicated time at the facility which is the first Monday of every month. It's a place every tourist should and must visit, packed with fun and bursting with life.

31. A DAY AT THE ZOO...

If i could adopt any zoo animal, it would be a parrot. you can never be bored with them around. Malmo Reptile Center is a cozy zoo located inside Folket park, with exotic reptiles, birds, animals and plants. This reptile center is better than any other in Sweden, the animals and cages are well maintained, spacious, inexpensive entrance fee and a small gift shop where you can buy nice toys for kids and odd collectibles for adults. you can't miss this place when you visit Malmo because it is located in one of the best parks in the city. There is an outdoor garden with birds where you relax while having fika. It's a kind of creepy place due to the spiders and snakes but the monkeys help in giving you a little comic relief. This zoo reminds me of a place I visited in 2011 called UShaka Marine World in Durban, South Africa. The place was filled with all kinds of snakes and spiders, and everything creepy. I still remember how scared my daughter was after the visit, but in all it was a great experience. The most fascinating part of Malmo Reptile Center are the Swedish speaking parrots; I just can't get over it.

32. JUST BREATHE....

Malmo is a city full of beautiful green spaces, trees, fresh air, no fumes, all you feel on your face is clean air. It's always nice taking a walk or riding a bike and feeling the air on your face while taking a breath of fresh clean air devoid of fumes. The city is not crowded like big cities and you don't see cars littering the place and traffic, it's an environment different from where I am coming from where the air slowly sends people to their early graves due to pollution. life in Malmo is different, so if you are visiting for the first time here is a tip for you, take it slow... Malmo is a place to relax and enjoy life at a slow pace, and not the hustle and bustle you find in most places.

33. STAY ON THE QUEUE.

There is something the city of Malmo has taught me and that is patience. everything is done in a slow and steady manner. There are processes involved in everything you do, you practically queue up for everything and wait patiently till it gets to your turn, there is much respect for individual space and even before the emergence of social distancing due to Coronavirus, it has been in practice since forever in Sweden especially in Malmo. If you are coming to Malmo to stay for a while and you want to rent an apartment for the short period, it is important that you arrange your accommodation before coming over. It is difficult to find rentals in Malmo especially in popular areas, you have to be on the queue, which is also on the waiting list, or go for a secondhand which is quite expensive or better still go to the nearby villages or cities. Before moving to Malmo I arranged for my accommodation while I was still in Nigeria, it helped me save money and time. A friend of mine who moved to Malmo without proper arrangements regretted it, she had to stay in Airbnb for almost 3 months before getting a place. be prepared always, while you wait patiently for your turn.

34. IT'S FRIDAY AND I'M READY TO SWING...

Nightlife in Malmo rivals that of Stockholm and Gothenburg. Malmo is not just a destination for history and nature but for late night. Tourists who like to party will get loads of it from Swedish pubs, dance clubs and karaoke bars, from midnight bowling to bustling disco, Malmo has got you covered. Nightlife in Malmo is best enjoyed during the weekends and always starts with a chill at the bar for a casual beer with your friends and then head to one of the high energy dance floors to party until wee hours in the morning. there are so many night clubs in Malmo, just have a chat with the locals and you will be directed to your choice, if you are straight or gay you have a place to fit in. tipping is not required or a custom in Sweden especially in Malmo. Alcohol is expensive in Sweden because sales are strictly regulated by the Government. so be prepared.

35. J-U-N-G-L-E

Malmo is a fun packed city, the name itself should be used to replace the Swedish word for fun. There is little of everything in this compact city and I can boldly say it is one of the best places to visit as a tourist. for those in love with the jungle, the city got you covered with Afrikaparken, a touch of Africa in Sweden, a place where you feel the jungle by taking a long walk in a crafted jungle with African sized animals in natural size, statues of giraffes, rhinos, elephants, crocodiles, all in life size. The best part of it are the funny tree animals hidden in the forest with mysterious jungle trails, good playground and adventurous climbing nets. My first visit there was awesome and I took lovely pictures that could actually pass for pictures taken in a real African jungle.

>TOURIST

36. I FOUND THE PERFECT GIFT.

For every trip we make we always look forward to the souvenirs we bring back home, not only for those we left at home but also for ourselves to constantly remind us of the places we have visited. If you take a look at my sitting room you can tell the places I have travelled to. I fell in love with souvenirs when I first visited Dubai. I had to pay for excess luggage due to amazing souvenirs I couldn't just let go. It is always good to bring something you've learned, or an outfit, or something you use every day in your kitchen, something for your wall or room decor or better still something priceless like a sea shell or stone. if you are visiting Malmo for the first time then you should be rest assured that you will be going home with breathtaking gifts for your friends, family and yourself. Malmo Clothing Co, a place where custom prints are done. If you want Malmo branded items to buy as souvenirs to take back to your country then you should visit this place, whether you are local or tourist. They have cheeky Malmo specific designs, like the Falafel sticker shirt and the turning torso designs et al. You can get them at very reasonable prices and in good quality. There are other shops where you can also get lovely Swedish souvenirs and most of these shops can be found in the parks or museums. don't forget to take something back home no matter how small for your loved ones and yourself to remind you of Malmo. it is not how much we give, but how much love we put into giving. - Mother Teresa.

37. ART IS WONDER...

The city of Malmo screams art everywhere you turn to. There are over 300 pieces of public arts from traditional to modern. If you love art, then the city of Malmo will definitely wow you in different ways. I love art and coming to Malmo has made it even more interesting to me. But of all the public arts, I have 2 favorites which I am going to recommend for you and maybe after you visit you will also have your own favorites and recommendations. MOTHER: this is first on my list, it was inaugurated in 2014 on the occasion of the Nordic forum. This sculpture is awe-inspiring. Each time I see it I am reminded of my experiences as a mother and my early morning

>TOURIST

sickness during pregnancy. It is a sculpture of the head of a woman whose face protrudes from the water of a large pool and a fountain of water shoots from her open mouth. It's a must see and can't be missed due to its location, but sadly it is difficult to get full effect because it is located in the middle of a traffic circle, getting a picture isn't so easy so i suggest you bring a drone so you can get that perfect view and picture. 2nd on my list is THE GIANT LAMP: it's a marvel to behold, unveiled in 2006 this 19-foot lamp has become a tourist, touring the various squares of the city throughout the year and from 15th December it stays in the popular Lilla Torg where it remains throughout the holiday season. The lamp gives passersby the opportunity to sit back and relax under it. the best part of it is that it actually talks… I know you are dying to know what it says, don't worry, a visit will help reveal that to you, *Spoilers Alert.

38. STICKING TO MY CANDY CRUSH.

Most people think candy crush addiction is real, certainly I agree with them. I love to play games, especially puzzle games. It takes me on an interesting journey. If you are a gamer and you are wondering if you can play in Malmo, am happy to introduce you to Escape Room Games in Malmo, where exciting adventures and great team games are available, to escape from a room within a given time or to complete a mission, its creepy and gives me chills. There are so many escape rooms in Malmo, Fox in a Box, Prison Island, The Alley, Sherlocked et al but I have never visited or tried playing because I have a phobia for escape rooms due to recent horror movies I have seen and how it always turns out real, you see participants fighting for their lives. for now, I only observe and dare not play…. A bit dramatic ?? may be. All you need to do is search for escape rooms in Malmo and you will find them, head to their pages and book a game for a very affordable price.

>TOURIST

39. BOOK A TOUR...

Malmo can be experienced in different ways as a tourist, whether you travel alone or in groups you can always find a way to have fun and make your visit a memorable one. let me walk you through this, you can book a custom tour by request with group of people riding through the city in a bus, or book a self-guided tour using the Malmo audio guide, or better still stick to the walking private tours with professional guides strolling through the city and lastly my favorite is Malmo bike tours which is ideal for summer, saddling and touring at the same time. and don't forget that Malmo is the best bike town in Sweden.

40. COUNT THE MEMORIES, NOT THE CALORIES.

One of my favorite things about Malmo is the food, the city has so much to offer and I like to try something new once in a while, if you are craving Thai noodles, Falafel, Samosas, and just about any food you can think of from the world, Malmo has it, a mix of modern and classic. if you are visiting for the first time and you love quality and mouth watering food from the melting pot of culture creativity and fun then I have just the destination for you, a warm welcome to a food lover's paradise, Malmo Saluhall, an upscale food hall where you can find any food, fruits, burger, noodles, falafel, ice-cream, salad, seafood and vegetarian options. It's a food market for everyone. you can enjoy your meal also in an outdoor street sitting, you really can't go wrong with anything here it's a must stop spot for visiting Malmo. The smell in there always gets me confused in making a choice on what to eat or where to eat from the numbers of different vendors. how can I forget to mention they sell the best Gelato in the whole of South Sweden? Malmo Saluhall is also a great place for solo travelers, you can eat, drink and wander until whenever. mind you, it's not cheap, you can already tell when you walk in, but hey!! you are traveling.

>TOURIST

41. RENT A CAR, AND EXPLORE.

If you are visiting Malmo alone or with your family and you need a vehicle to take a tour round the city, there is always something for you in all shapes and sizes. Renting a car in Malmo is as easy as ABC, but here are some tips for you before renting one in order to avoid fines and also to make your driving a smooth one in the city. If you decide to rent or bring your personal car down for your trip you must follow these simple guidelines. your headlight must always be switched on even in daytime, you must have the right tyres for each season, parking is difficult and expensive in the city, you may want to park at your hotel or book parking facility in advance, most roadside parking is paid for at the ticket machines and you must display your ticket. I've got good news for you, there are no toll roads in Malmo, but you may be charged to cross Oresund Bridge. The first time I rented a car I took a trip to Lund which is 20km away from Malmo and it was a jolly ride with my course mates. The process was easy at Europcar, one of the best in Malmo, with over 5 stations in the city, the car was delivered to me and when I was done they came for pickup, it was such a lovely experience. you should try renting a car when you visit and don't forget to obey the traffic lights.

42. A QUIET TIME AND PLACE.

Touted as Sweden's marvel, where the old joins the new, this elegant and classic ancient design leaves you marveled at her beauty, a 14th century Architectural masterpiece right in the middle of the city, this beautiful aesthetic building offers a perfect environment to make a pause and pray and also have a few quiet moments to yourself. it's definitely worth a visit if you like hundreds of years of history in front of you. No wonder the New National Geographic Travel named Malmo one of its best trips of 2018. A visit to Malmo and not stepping foot in St Peter's Church (St Petri Kyrka) is an error, this city church is one of the oldest buildings in Malmo which is regarded as the wealth of Swedish history with an interesting combination of old and new elements inside. 5 minutes' walk from central park, there is really no excuse not to see it if you are visiting Malmo. Each time I visit this beauty it boggles my mind how man could craft such a monumental structure with bare hands. a nice place for great pictures and you are always welcomed.

43. A SLICE OF CULTURE, CUSTOMS AND ETIQUETTE.

If you reject the food, ignore the customs, fear the religion and avoid the people, you might better stay at home. - James Michener. A slice of Swedish hospitality is a very common practice in Malmo/Sweden, dining with locals in order to learn their customs and culture. It offers visitors a chance to discover everyday life in the city. This is for sure the most authentic way of experiencing Malmo from the words of people who have lived there all their lives. You can embrace this by booking a time to spend with any family of your choice from the list and have a chance to be hosted, while you ask questions about culture and traditions and inside tips on what to see and where to shop in Malmo. mind you, it's not free, all you have to do is send a request and you will be guided on how to go about it. Please note that host families decide dates and numbers of persons.

Swedish are extremely punctual people especially at meals.

44. THE MOST EXPENSIVE NOISE.

As a thespian I have always loved the theatre and everything that has to do with live performances, and my favorite is the opera. If you are a fan of musical drama, then Malmo Opera should be the best place for you while visiting Malmö. It is the largest auditorium in Scandinavia with 1508 seats. built in 1930 but yet it looks modern. a great place to spend an afternoon or evening, easy to access by train and car with easy parking. Each time I visit it reminds me of the movie "Phantom of The Opera", such a great movie. you cannot say you have been to Malmo and not visited this wonderful building to enjoy a show with great performances, comfortable seats, good view, fantastic place for kids, great food, great acoustic, and best shows, the one that got everyone talking was the Beauty and the Beast show, I can't forget that in a hurry. Did I mention that as a student you get 50% off? ok!! I just did.

>TOURIST

45. EITHER GIVE ME MORE WINE OR LEAVE ME ALONE. - RUMI

Drinking wine and Netflixing has become a Saturday night fun ritual for me. I love wine. No, like I really love wine and my favorite is white wine due to the calmness it gives you after a hectic day. My next vacation will definitely be in Italy, my dream location where i will have to go on a wine tasting spree and try the famous Italian pizza, spaghetti and gelato, but before I go on that trip let me first inform you that you can also get all of this in Malmo at the Gustavino Malmo and Ciao Malmo. fantastic place if you want to enjoy Italy in Malmo. great place for Italian dishes and wine lovers. located in the heart of the city with great ambience and decorations, high quality yet affordable continental charm with a warm and friendly environment where you can have fun with your friend while you go on a wine tasting tour. you can also practice or learn your Italian at the bar while enjoying your happy hour. For beer lovers you can visit Malmo Brewing Company where you find different selections of beer, imported and locally made, all served from a tap. it's a great place to visit while in Malmo. Have you ever tried cheese and wine? you should, it's such a mad combo.

46. WE ARE ALL MAD HERE.

Festivals make us look crazy sometimes, it's like a license to misbehave and go wild for a few hours. if you want to see crazy and at same time go wild for a while then you should try visiting Malmo during the month of August and have a long week of culture, food, music and entertainment that sprawls across the city with free performances from Swedish celebrities in the famous and most anticipated gathering called Malmo Festival (Malmofestivalen), which is usually organized by the Municipality of Malmo and it was founded in 1985. make your vacation unforgettable by having a taste of this festival. Malmo is a natural hub for people and culture from around the world so be sure to see fun in diverse ways.

>TOURIST

47. LET'S GO GET SOME GROCERIES.

My favorite day is Saturday when I have to be at home with my family and the best part of the day is going out with my family to get groceries, my kids always look forward to Saturdays, because it's a day to refill the refrigerator and also go out and have a bit of fun running through the shop. In Malmo grocery shopping is always fun and if you are new in the city here are some tips for you. try shopping at international stores, they are the best in terms of price. Sweden does have a large number of big brands named stores but they are expensive, the local international stores have unbeatable prices and these stores range from Asian stores to Lebanese and Syrians. but if you don't mind the cost then you can ICA and COOP they are everywhere in town and can't be missed. Malmö is said to be the food basket of Sweden and this is the best part of it. You can get fresh veggies and fruits straight from the farm at the farmer's market on Saturday mornings at a very small cost. There is something I noticed in Malmo after purchasing an item most cashiers will ask if you need a receipt, I always wonder why? Please always request for one.

48. CHOCO. LA. TA.

Let's take a trip to Malmo ChokladFabrik. For my chocolate enthusiasts this place is highly recommended, the great chocolate museum and boutique shop is an extraordinary small chocolate factory where organic chocolate is made. They hold chocolate tasting and tours all year except in July. even non chocolate lovers will fall in love and it's a suitable souvenir to take back home. I still remember my first visit there and for the first time I tasted the best chocolate to any other I have tried, and all their products are nut free, truly a real gem in Malmo but it's on the high side so be prepared.

49. SWEDISH IDENTITY.

A trip to Malmo without setting a foot in Ikea is an error. Ikea is one of Swedish identity founded in Sweden 1943 by a 17 years old Ingvar Kamprad, and

>TOURIST

the world's largest furniture retailer. a paradise for everyone who either wants to enjoy good food at a very reasonable price or who would like to have a one stop house decor shopping item for each and every corner of their house. When I moved to Malmo I got everything in my house from Ikea, ranging from furniture, kitchen utensils, beddings and my best part are the live plants. Each trip I take to Ikea I go back home with a live plant. Ikea is a community of its own, so huge, colorful and filled with everything you can ever imagine in a home with beautiful designs which are more towards greener decorations. you can't go home empty handed once you get in, and please go with a credit card because cash is hardly accepted and also be ready to do lots of translations because most of the instructions are written in Swedish. After shopping you can visit their restaurant. It's the cheapest place to buy food in Malmo with great Swedish traditional food and they make the best meatballs in the city. Sorry I can't help it; I love good food. Ikea is the best place for students and tourists, because everything is easy, and cheap to get.

50. DANCING ROUND THE MAYPOLE.

Midsummer is the biggest and best celebration in Sweden, which is usually celebrated in June 20-26. Most people in the cities go to the countryside to celebrate hereby leaving the cities empty and deserted. but in Malmo it's a different vibe entirely, if you happen to be in Malmo during the celebration then all you have to do is head to Folkets Park and there you will experience the maypole dance and a taste of festivity. The maypole is a symbol of fertility and it is erected at popular gatherings across the country. where dancing and drinking into the night is done. It's such a great time to visit Sweden, especially Malmo. The first time I saw people dancing round a maypole it was spooky and strange but now i find it rather interesting and it has become my 2nd best celebration after Christmas, the most interesting part of the celebration is the part where young women are supposed to pick up 7 different species of flowers and lay them under their pillows with the believe that at night their future husbands will appear to them…. ok!! Now this is creepy.

>TOURIST

TOP REASONS TO BOOK THIS TRIP

If you are a daring and wildly adventurous person and have a large taste for multicultural hospitality, then you need to see the fantastic options that Malmo offers. This compendium offers you a budget cut size hospitality in one of the calmest places in Europe, trust me, you don't have to break the bank to make this trip a reality and also get the best value for your money.

Beaches: The beaches here are the best, with great options and wild fun.

Food: The food is amazing, with a wide range of delicacies. and the mouthwatering humble ball of fried chickpeas called Falafel which has become a symbol for Malmo.

Beautiful parks and Art: There are so many beautiful parks, street arts and museums of all kinds to explore with different varieties from traditional to modern and from the old to the new.

I hope this little guide will help any budding traveler planning to take a trip to Malmo.

>TOURIST

PACKING AND PLANNING TIPS

A Week before Leaving

- Arrange for someone to take care of pets and water plants.
- Email and Print important Documents.
- Get Visa and vaccines if needed.
- Check for travel warnings.
- Stop mail and newspaper.
- Notify Credit Card companies where you are going.
- Passports and photo identification is up to date.
- Pay bills.
- Copy important items and download travel Apps.
- Start collecting small bills for tips.
- Have post office hold mail while you are away.
- Check weather for the week.
- Car inspected, oil is changed, and tires have the correct pressure.
- Check airline luggage restrictions.
- Download Apps needed for your trip.

Right Before Leaving

- Contact bank and credit cards to tell them your location.
- Clean out refrigerator.
- Empty garbage cans.
- Lock windows.
- Make sure you have the proper identification with you.
- Bring cash for tips.
- Remember travel documents.
- Lock door behind you.
- Remember wallet.
- Unplug items in house and pack chargers.
- Change your thermostat settings.
- Charge electronics, and prepare camera memory cards.

>TOURIST

READ OTHER GREATER THAN A TOURIST BOOKS

Greater Than a Tourist- California: 50 Travel Tips from Locals

Greater Than a Tourist- Salem Massachusetts USA 50 Travel Tips from a Local by Danielle Lasher

Greater Than a Tourist United States: 50 Travel Tips from Locals

Greater Than a Tourist- St. Croix US Birgin Islands USA: 50 Travel Tips from a Local by Tracy Birdsall

Greater Than a Tourist- Montana: 50 Travel Tips from a Local by Laurie White

Children's Book: Charlie the Cavalier Travels the World by Lisa Rusczyk Ed. D.

> TOURIST

Follow us on Instagram for beautiful travel images:
http://Instagram.com/GreaterThanATourist

Follow *Greater Than a Tourist* on Amazon.

CZYKPublishing.com

> TOURIST

At *Greater Than a Tourist*, we love to share travel tips with you. How did we do? What guidance do you have for how we can give you better advice for your next trip? Please send your feedback to GreaterThanaTourist@gmail.com as we continue to improve the series. We appreciate your constructive feedback. Thank you.

>TOURIST

METRIC CONVERSIONS

TEMPERATURE

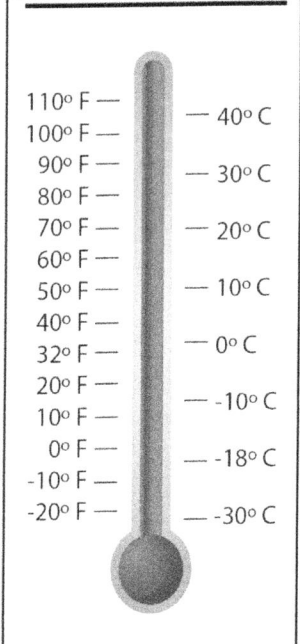

- 110° F — 40° C
- 100° F
- 90° F — 30° C
- 80° F
- 70° F — 20° C
- 60° F
- 50° F — 10° C
- 40° F
- 32° F — 0° C
- 20° F
- 10° F — -10° C
- 0° F
- -10° F — -18° C
- -20° F — -30° C

To convert F to C:

Subtract 32, and then multiply by 5/9 or .5555.

To Convert C to F:

Multiply by 1.8 and then add 32.

32F = 0C

LIQUID VOLUME

To Convert:................Multiply by
U.S. Gallons to Liters................ 3.8
U.S. Liters to Gallons 26
Imperial Gallons to U.S. Gallons 1.2
Imperial Gallons to Liters....... 4.55
Liters to Imperial Gallons 22

1 Liter = .26 U.S. Gallon
1 U.S. Gallon = 3.8 Liters

DISTANCE

To convert ....Multiply by
Inches to Centimeters 2.54
Centimeters to Inches 39
Feet to Meters...................... .3
Meters to Feet 3.28
Yards to Meters 91
Meters to Yards 1.09
Miles to Kilometers 1.61
Kilometers to Miles............ .62

1 Mile = 1.6 km
1 km = .62 Miles

WEIGHT

1 Ounce = .28 Grams
1 Pound = .4555 Kilograms
1 Gram = .04 Ounce
1 Kilogram = 2.2 Pounds

>TOURIST

TRAVEL QUESTIONS

- Do you bring presents home to family or friends after a vacation?
- Do you get motion sick?
- Do you have a favorite billboard?
- Do you know what to do if there is a flat tire?
- Do you like a sun roof open?
- Do you like to eat in the car?
- Do you like to wear sun glasses in the car?
- Do you like toppings on your ice cream?
- Do you use public bathrooms?
- Did you bring a cell phone and does it have power?
- Do you have a form of identification with you?
- Have you ever been pulled over by a cop?
- Have you ever given money to a stranger on a road trip?
- Have you ever taken a road trip with animals?
- Have you ever gone on a vacation alone?
- Have you ever run out of gas?

- If you could move to any place in the world, where would it be?
- If you could travel anywhere in the world, where would you travel?
- If you could travel in any vehicle, which one would it be?
- If you had three things to wish for from a magic genie, what would they be?
- If you have a driver's license, how many times did it take you to pass the test?
- What are you the most afraid of on vacation?
- What do you want to get away from the most when you are on vacation?
- What foods smell bad to you?
- What item do you bring on ever trip with you away from home?
- What makes you sleepy?
- What song would you love to hear on the radio when you're cruising on the highway?
- What travel job would you want the least?
- What will you miss most while you are away from home?
- What is something you always wanted to try?

>TOURIST

- What is the best road side attraction that you ever saw?
- What is the farthest distance you ever biked?
- What is the farthest distance you ever walked?
- What is the weirdest thing you needed to buy while on vacation?
- What is your favorite candy?
- What is your favorite color car?
- What is your favorite family vacation?
- What is your favorite food?
- What is your favorite gas station drink or food?
- What is your favorite license plate design?
- What is your favorite restaurant?
- What is your favorite smell?
- What is your favorite song?
- What is your favorite sound that nature makes?
- What is your favorite thing to bring home from a vacation?
- What is your favorite vacation with friends?
- What is your favorite way to relax?
- Where is the farthest place you ever traveled in a car?

- Where is the farthest place you ever went North, South, East and West?
- Where is your favorite place in the world?
- Who is your favorite singer?
- Who taught you how to drive?
- Who will you miss the most while you are away?
- Who if the first person you will contact when you get to your destination?
- Who brought you on your first vacation?
- Who likes to travel the most in your life?
- Would you rather be hot or cold?
- Would you rather drive above, below, or at the speed limited?
- Would you rather drive on a highway or a back road?
- Would you rather go on a train or a boat?
- Would you rather go to the beach or the woods?

>TOURIST

TRAVEL BUCKET LIST

1.

2.

3.

4.

5.

6.

7.

8.

9.

10.

>TOURIST

NOTES

Printed in Great Britain
by Amazon